Groundhogs

Woodchucks and other Marmots

Dr. Richard A. NeSmith

Love of Nature Series

ISSUE 34

Applied **P**rinciples of **E**ducation & *Learning*

APE-Learning

© 2021 Richard A. NeSmith
Love of Nature Series

dr.nesmith@gmail.com

http://richardnesmith.obior.cc

Dr. Richard A. NeSmith

MAY 2025

ISBN: 9798733038278

FLESCH-KINCAID GRADE LEVEL: 8.4

Groundhogs

(Marmota *monax*)

Can a **groundhog** foretell the weather? Can a **woodchuck** chuck wood? In all likelihood, the answer to both is negative. If they could, then both could do so, for they are both the same animal. They are **rodents**[1] belonging to a group of tree squirrels and are the largest *ground squirrels* known as **marmots**.[2] Marmots are one of the largest members of the squirrel family. And, we will see that many of their cousins look very similar, though living in different habitats.

Groundhogs are a single group of animals with a variety of regional names and identities. It is also referred to as a chuck, wood-shock, ground pig, whistlepig, land beaver,

The groundhog greetings is for one to place their nose up at the mouth of the other.

---

[1] Of the family Sciuridae. Rodents make up about 40% of all mammal species.

[2] Groundhogs are one of 14 species of marmots (Marmota), considered basically a giant North American ground squirrel.

whistler, thickwood badger, red monk, rock chuck, mouse bear, Canada marmot, monax, moonack, weenusk, and, among French Canadians in eastern Canada, siffleux.

We have considered in earlier issues of the *Love of Nature* series how common names can create confusion and issues. So, we have one specific scientific name for all animals and organisms found. These large ground squirrels were first described scientifically by none other than Carolus Linnaeus, himself the father of scientific classification. In 1758 AD, he called them Marmota *monax*.[3] Marmota means *mountain mouse*. The common name *Móonack* is an Algonquian word meaning "digger," and now shortened to be Monax. So, all of these same animals with various common names are identified as the single genus-species

---

[3] Scientific names are bionomial (meaning two names), and include the genus and species of an organism which permits anyone in the world to be able to discuss only this one animal without confusion.

Marmota[4] *monax*. The groundhog species in the Western
United States include the Yellow-bellied Marmot (Marmota

---

[4] Some believe the name Marmota originates from some of the old romance languages, where the prefix *marm-*, means to *mumble* or *murmur*.

flaviventris).

The first question posed was whether groundhogs could *chuck wood*? The second was whether a groundhog could *predict the weather*? These questions arise from two fascinating legends surrounding these questions. First, "woodchuck" actually is not wood at all: Instead, it may be

addressing:

a) the possible fact that the woodchuck eats plants and,

b) its practice of digging, referred to as chucking (presumably the dirt flying out of the den digging in the process).

Then there is the classical children's Mother Goose nursery rhyme, asking the question.

> *How much wood could a woodchuck chuck*
> *If a woodchuck could chuck wood?*
> *As much wood as a woodchuck could chuck,*
> *If a woodchuck could chuck wood.*

Finally, we recognize the strange trivia fact that groundhogs are the only animals in the United States that have their own holiday, **Groundhog Day**,[5] every February 2nd. The idea centers around the groundhog leaving its den on that day, and if it sees its shadow, there will be six more weeks of winter. By the way, the accuracy rate of the famous Punxsutawney Phil in Pennsylvania[6] has been about 35 to 40%. This fact might simply suggest that rodents do not make great prognosticators or weather forecasters.[7]

Range

Marmots live on three continents. They are found in Asia, Europe, and North America. These animals make their homes in mountainous areas, meadows, tundra, forest

---

[5] 1887 A.D. Some have suggested this actually may have orginated from ancient European beliefs that badgers and hedgehogs can provide signals about the future.

[6] There already was a significant holiday in the German communities in Pennsylvania prior to this which focused on a feast, called Candlemas. It included that if the weather was clear on Febrruary 2nd then the winter would contine for six more weeks. However, if it was cloudy, then spring would arrive early. By 1840, the groundhog was included in this celebration.

[7] Granted, professional weather forecasters are typical accurate 80-90% of the time.

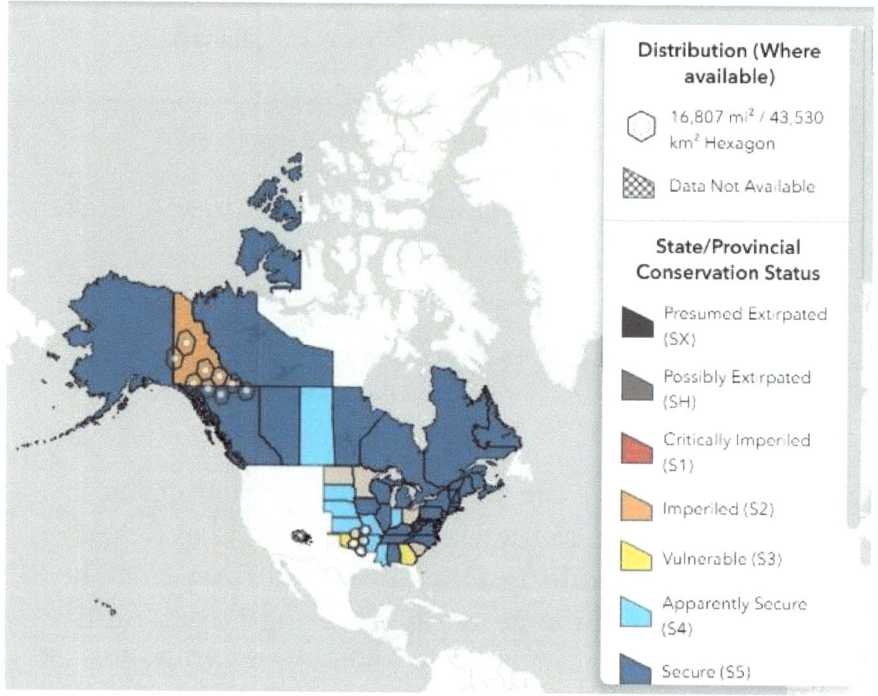

edges, grasslands, and steppes.

Groundhogs are widely distributed across North America, and most are lowland creatures. Some highland marmots live in the Rocky Mountains, the Sierra Nevada, and the Olympic Mountains in Washington State.

Marmots are found *throughout* most of the United States, Canada, and southern Alaska. Groundhogs are generally located in most eastern and central States and southern Canada, through southern Yukon and the Northwest Territories. They can range as far south as northern Alabama, Georgia, South Carolina, and north to Maine and even Alaska. Some communities seem to have large populations of woodchucks, such as in New England, where woodchucks inhabit both urban and suburban yards,[8] fields, meadows, woodland clearings, and grassy areas along highways. In some regions, they are prolific and can average one woodchuck per 4000 people.[9] This is not common, and population numbers depend significantly on *habitat quality*.[10]

The exact population of eastern groundhogs and the western yellow-bellied marmots is unknown. They are often found in Colorado, Utah, Nevada, New Mexico, California, Oregon, Washington State, and Alaska.[11] The National Parks have large populations, including the Rocky

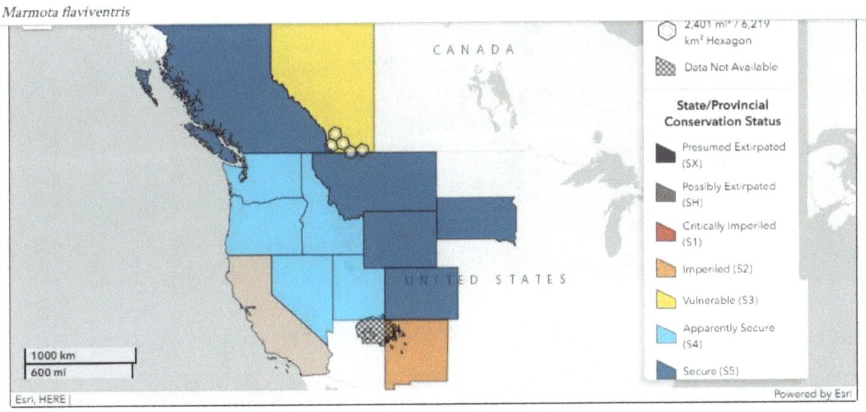

Mountain National Park in Colorado, Sequoia & Kings Canyon in California, Olympic National Park in Washington State, and Denali National Park and Reserve in

---

[8] Though the yellow-bellied marmot avoids residential areas.

[9] Population counts are rare and regionally distinct. Some studies have suggested that the western yellow-bellied marmots have recorded population densities ranges from 0.04 to 1.3 individuals per acre (0.1 to 3.3 individuals per hectare).

[10] Woodchuck numbers vary from area to area, depend- ing on food availability, soil type, hunting pressure, and predation. Sometimes populations are highly dense, with up to six or seven individuals per acre; this high density is seldom reached.

[11] Smaller populations have been identified in most of the western states. The same can be said of most of the central states.

Alaska, to name just a few!

We will see that a woodchuck's range depends on its required habitat, which necessitates ample access to forests and the need for a true winter season. And, of course,

adequate food sources. If you noticed from the maps, the central part of the US heartland is not significantly populated by woodchucks; however, the prairie dog relatives have filled that niche.

Because groundhogs are mammals, let us briefly review the characteristics that all mammals share in common.

INTRODUCTION TO MAMMALS

Groundhogs are mammals. Mammals are a well-known class of vertebrates that includes 5,000 species (of which 14 species are marmots). As mammals, they are warm-blooded (**endotherms**), which creates their own body heat, mainly

from liver **metabolism**. They possess **hair** or fur. They have a wholly divided **four-chambered heart** for efficient circulation and thus have sufficient mobility on command. They have an upper and lower jaw and have **specialized teeth**, especially *incisors*, which continue to grow throughout their lifespan. They possess **milk glands** and provide *care* **for their young**.

Characteristics

Woodchucks are rotund and cuddling-looking animals with small earflaps and a black nose. Their ears and nose can be contracted closed to prevent dirt from entering when digging dens or burrows, called cettes (pronounced "sets"). Some say they more closely resemble a bear than a squirrel,

Mocha meets a new little friend and shares five minutes together.

especially when they stand up on their short, muscular hind legs. They have long and sharp curved claws (on four front toes and five back toes).[12] These make for great digging, and their burrows are very impressive structures.

A groundhog (Marmota *monax*) is a rodent and a rather

---

[12] Technically these "fingers" are called *digits*.

large one at that. From head to rump, adult groundhogs are often 17 to 24 inches (43 to 61 centimeters) long. They can weigh 14 lbs. (6.4 kilograms). This size is about twice the average weight of a newborn human baby! Currently, Ohio claims the record for the largest woodchuck at 16 pounds (7.3 kg).

Like other squirrels, they have long, bushy, furry tails. The tail can grow to seven to ten inches (18 to 25 cm) long. Being a marmot makes it closely related to chipmunks, squirrels of all kinds, rats, mice, prairie dogs, and even

Yellow-bellied marmot from the Grand Tetons.

beavers.[13] Like squirrels, it spins and lifts its tail as it runs,

---

[13] See Love of Nature series 9 entitled, *Beavers: Nature's Engineers!* (2020), also, series 7, Squirrels: Bushy-Tail Scampers! (2020).

and being so chunky, it runs surprisingly fast if excited (8 miles per hour/12.9 kph). However, their greatest defense against predators is a *fast retreat* to their underground den.

Habitat

Groundhogs dig burrows that can be 6 feet (1.8 meters) deep and 20 feet (6 meters) wide and often have multiple entrances and exits. These caves can be 66 feet (20.1 m) long.[14] Winter burrows tend to be deeper underground for warmth-control reasons. Since most of the United States' frost line is no more than eight feet below the ground surface, the temperature stays consistently above freezing (32°F/0°C) and averages above 50°F (10°C). Not all

---

[14] Some report they have found burrows up to 80 feet long (more then three-fourths the length of an American gridiron football field.

burrows are occupied.[15]

Woodchucks are the number one *hole-digging* mammal of eastern North America. It is estimated that marmots spend 80% of their life below ground. This fact might explain how some of their burrows are quite extensive. The average groundhog can excavate over 700 pounds of dirt while digging a single den. One groundhog can have four or five dens scattered across its territory, relocating according to crop availability and weather conditions.

According to the National Wildlife Federation, underground groundhog homes can have two to a dozen different entrances. These are sometimes hidden or camouflaged with grasses or shrubs, or most often below a stump or large rock. An escape hole or two is concealed in nearby vegetation. The dens' openings are usually relatively small (7-8 inches; 17.8-20.3 cm), which keeps larger animals

---

[15] In one study, 75% of active burrows were found to house permanent residents.

from entering. However, as with rodents, the groundhog has no problem squeezing through tight places, even with their chubby body. Typically, they have a burrow in the forest for the winter and a den in grassy areas during the warmer months. Groundhogs are pretty clean animals and keep their cave dens tidy by changing their nesting grasses, hay, and leaves inside from time to time. Burrows have a nest chamber lined with dead leaves and dried grass and several blind pockets which serve as designated latrines (toilet chambers). They groom their fur coats frequently.

Groundhogs are known as being **edge species**. This phrase means that groundhogs prefer transitional areas where forest or woodland meets a well-vegetated open field or meadow. ***Edge habitats*** are **ecotones**[16] found where one habitat type joins another. One example would be

---

[16] An ecotone is an area that acts as a boundary or a transition between two ecosystems.

where the tree line of a forest meets a farm field, creating an edge. They can be found along grassy highway rights-of-way and utility corridors, all of which provide habitat for woodchucks.

Edge habitats are prevalent and are used by many wildlife species for food and shelter. Migrating species also use these areas for food, shelter, and rest. Edge habitats are vital because they are not just a transition between two ecosystems (also called **biomes**), but because they have a large variety of **fauna** and **flora**, which also influences *both* borderline ecosystems.

When outside their den, groundhogs are usually searching for food, sunning, or standing guard. One of their greatest defenses is being stealthy. They are quiet, and when motionless, are almost impossible to see. The yellow-bellied marmots take turns standing guard over a colony like a sentry. This shrill sound alarms the other marmots, upon which they quickly scurry off into their holes. They also communicate with chattering and clicking noises and occasionally what sounds like a scream.

Diet

Groundhogs are **herbivores** and eat vegetation.[17] They are very fond of fruits, plants, flowers, nuts, grains, clover, goldenrods, asters, apples, and berries. They consume buds and bark of deciduous trees and shrubs, and various grasses. They occasionally eat insects, including grasshoppers. They eat what is seasonally plentiful in their range during spring and summer. This voracious appetite can create problems for farmers and gardeners, as they love field crops and can cause considerable damage in a very short period. Like other rodents, some woodchucks have been known to eat particular poisonous plants without

---

[17] Biology specialist refer to them more specifically as folivores and granivore. A folivore eats a lot of leaves and a granivore eats the seeds of plants.

being affected.[18]

Like all rodents, their incisor teeth continue to grow throughout their lives. The incisors can grow up to one inch in four months. However, they are constantly grinding those teeth down. These teeth are angled so that the top

rubs against the bottom teeth, keeping them sharpened like a knife.

The teeth are also arranged to give the groundhog a *whistling* sound, a defense mechanism often heard when feeling threatened or when warning other groundhogs of potential danger. This shrill screech sound is also the source for the common name "whistle-pig." They do

---

[18] Most poisonous plants can indeed harm or kill a woodchuck, for like all rodents, woodchucks lack the gag response or the esophageal muscles to be able to regurgitate (vomit) such food eaten. They are, in fact, being used by medical research to determine how to help human cancer patients to not become nauseous during treatment.

communicate with one another.

According to the National Wildlife Federation, the groundhog's teeth grow at a rate of a sixteenth of an inch (1.6 millimeters) each week during the warm months. Like beavers, hamsters, or other rodents, should the groundhog not wear down its teeth continually, the top incisors would overgrow the bottom ones, and the animal would eventually die from starvation. This situation typically does not occur in nature, as these mammals have voracious appetites. This is especially so after immediately coming out of hibernation and the beginning of autumn, when they need to put on the extra fat for hibernation.

Hibernation

Hibernation is triggered by several factors in an animal, including *decreasing day length* and *hormonal changes*. These dictate the need to conserve energy. This creates an insatiable drive to simply *live to eat*. Some have called this a

feast-or-famine lifestyle. As a result, these rodents weigh more in the fall season than they do in the spring, namely because they eat so much over summer and early autumn, building up fat levels to such that they could hibernate for three to six months if needed.[19] Groundhogs begin hibernating from late fall, depending on their region, and it generally will last up to 150 days. But when they first awake, it can still be quite cold.

Though for the eastern woodchuck, hibernation is an isolated event, yellow-bellied marmots huddle together in a burrow for warmth. It is not entirely uncommon that other animals (even snakes[20]) might join a den to share body heat.

Hibernation is entirely a **metabolic** change that saves energy. Upon entering hibernation, there is a drop in the woodchuck's body temperature to as low as 35 degrees

---

19 There are some reports of hibernation lasting several months longer.
20 See Love of Nature, Issue 21, *Non-venomous Snakes: Slithering Reptiles* (2020).

Fahrenheit (1.7°C)![21] Blood freezes at 31.0°F (-0.6°C). That is near-death levels. The heart rate drops from the normal rate of 80 beats per minute to 4–10 beats per minute. The breathing rate falls to one breath every six minutes. During hibernation, they can experience torpor and arousal periods, but it is not a frequent event. Some have witnessed woodchucks out of the den at various times during winter. Because stored fat-burning (metabolizing) does produce a minimal amount of waste, some thought is that this may

---

[21] In comparisoin, humans go into mild *hypothermia* when their body temperature drops a mere 3 degrees, lose consciousness at 82 degrees and face death below 70 degrees.

bring on very short periods of brief activity.[22]

The amount of weight put on for winter hibernation is critical for survival. It is estimated that juvenile males need at least seven pounds of additional fat and six for females. Less than this, and they will not survive. By the end of hibernation, the woodchuck will have lost as much as 25 to 40% of its beginning body weight.

Hibernation comes at a high cost. The woodchuck is entirely helpless during this stage. It will have reduced sensory and motor functions. This leads to increased potential danger from predators. Also, it reduces **protein synthesis**,[23] causes sleep deprivation, and decreases **immune** responses. Sleeping through winter may sound like a piece of cake. It is, however, a dangerous and challenging time of survival without one's normal defenses.

---

[22] Most food content eaten prior to hibernation has already passed out of the woodchuck before the deep sleep occurs.
[23] The process in which cells make proteins.

Biologists refer to this as a cost-benefit factor that increases the likelihood of survival.

In February, male woodchucks leave the hibernation den searching for the burrows of females'. This February

resurfacing for a short period fits well with the **Groundhog Day** legend. When a potential mate is found, he enters and introduces himself to possible mates (pre-courtship). He may even stay the night, though too early for breeding to occur. It is believed this might be a time of bonding between the potential mates. The male will then return to his den and go back to sleep for another month or until it is time to mate.

A few woodchucks migrate to various locations, from their winter dens to their summer dens. Typically, winter dens are created at lower altitudes than the summer ones.

Reproduction

Male groundhogs, called **he-chucks,** are slightly larger than

females (**she-chucks**). The eastern groundhogs are **solitary** creatures, except during mating season. The western species are more social and form family groups, creating colonies.[24]

Males are also very **territorial,** and their areas do not overlap. It is not uncommon for two or three females to overlap a male's territory. Groundhogs of both sexes mark their territory with **scent glands** (chemical communications) to warn others away from the area. It may be urine or rubbing their oil glands against various objects, plants, rocks, or trees. Though a marmot's territory will vary in size based on food availability, this can sometimes include up to seven acres of land, or much less, depending on the marmot population.

Yellow-bellied marmots, however, in the western USA are more **social** and live within colonies of 10-20 individuals. These western groundhogs from the family colony get along reasonably well. But, if an animal from another colony enters a strange burrow, there can be fights between the males. They chase and fiercely bite one another over

---

[24] It seems there is no word describing a group of marmots. Animals creating such coloinies are said to be mutualistic, as they assist one aother for survival.

territory.

Though territories are established, male and female groundhogs can occupy and overlap the same territories year after year. There is minimal overlap between home ranges for females except for the late spring and early summer, as females try to expand their territories.

The mating season starts in early March. This timing is perfect since food becomes more abundant as plants and tree buds begin to refoliate with new, tender leaves. Remember, the woodchucks have lost up to 40% of their pre-hibernation weight. And, though just awakening, they already become eating machines and start packing on the body fat they'll need for the next winter ahead. Females welcome a litter of perhaps a half-dozen newborns, which stay with their mother for several months. The mating

season progresses, and two to eight offspring are born after a gestation period of approximately 30 to 32 days. But the average is four live healthy newborns.

Baby woodchucks are called **pups**, **kits**, or **cubs** and are usually born in April. Kits born in the **natal** burrow are pink, hairless, and about one tablespoon's size, and weigh about one ounce. Their ears are folded, and their eyes are still closed. The babies are very sensitive to temperature and cluster next to their mother for warmth. If they should wander a little, they can find their way back to the nest by scent and by the heat given off by the bodies of their littermates and mother. They are quite the snug-in-a-rug bug, and the most severe threat they have during this stage is snakes. Snakes can detect their scent and movements through the ground and will come right through the front door of the burrow. Mother groundhogs have been known to defend their babies bravely, even killing and eat invading snakes. The kits communicate with their mother with soft squeaking noises and cry louder if they are hungry or cold. By four weeks, they are furred and their eyes open. Young remain in the burrow for 20-30 days.

Infants get mom's assistance for two to three months after birth. This maternal care may be the reason that survival rates appear to be relatively high for marmots. The natal burrow is the birthing chamber. It is usually only about three times the mother's length to retain warmth and help her keep her babies close. As they outgrow the natal burrow, the mother will move them to other dens. Around August, most chucklings have dispersed and left, seeking their own territories.

Dispersal is a vulnerable time for woodchucks, as their lack of experience can prove fatal. However, about 35% of female offspring will stay around longer, usually leaving the

home area after their first birthday or before their mother produces a new litter.

The western yellow-bellied marmot creates family social groups consisting of one adult male and two adult females. Each has offspring from the previous breeding season (usually female chucklings) and the current litter of infants.[25] Interactions within a female group are generally *friendly*. But interactions between female groups - even when the same adult male shares in those groups - are rare and aggressive. Though daddy woodchucks do not live at home from the breeding season through the first month of the infants' lives, he visits each of his female groups every day.

The yellow-bellied marmot's breeding season takes place a little later than the eastern species, from May to June. These animals breed just once per year. Olympic marmots

---

[25] This practice is very similar to what is found with squirrel and beaver relatives.

breed every other year.

Male marmots mate with several females during this time (called **harem polygynous**). He is protective and defends/guards them from other male marmots. Likewise, females mate with more than one male, so kits in the same litter often have different fathers.

The mother nurses her pups for about three weeks then begins feeding them grasses and plants. The pups begin to venture out of the burrow to explore and look for food at around four weeks old. They are fully weaned at five to seven weeks of age. Though the female continues to care of the kits by bringing them green vegetation to eat, they grow quickly and become more self-sufficient. At this time, the adolescent woodchuck is called a **chuckling**.

In some cases, the parents of 7-week-old pups will chase

chucklings away from the colony, forcing them to find a new system of burrows in which to live. Chucklings are sexually mature at about two years of age. They eventually set up their own territories and reproduced offspring.

Behavior

Groundhogs are **diurnal**, meaning they are active during the daylight hours. They spend most of their time in summer and autumn, continually feeding and napping in the sun. When they are not relaxing in their cave, they spend time relaxing and sunning themselves on rocks to get warm. The keyword seems to be *relaxing*. That is just a bit of an overstatement because they have such an appetite that they eat frequently. In each meal, they consume about one pound (0.454 kg) of food. In comparison, that is equivalent to a 150-pound human eating a 15-pound steak! This craving and gluttony are really out of necessity.

Groundhogs do communicate with one another. They greet each other with a type of Eskimo kiss. One groundhog approaches and touches its nose to the mouth of the second groundhog. Scientists call this "naso-oral contact."

Groundhogs are not wanderers but rather are homebodies. They typically stick close to home and tend to be very cautious animals, easily frightened. According to the Internet Center for Wildlife Damage Management, they usually don't wander farther than 50 to 150 feet (15 to 30 m) from their den during the daytime.

Groundhogs can be aggressive by nature. But that is generally true of any wild animal that becomes afraid or is challenged. And they can sometimes be destructive to gardens and pasturelands. They are known for damaging crops and gardens, and that is why many people consider them pests.

Hibernation

People often get very confused when it comes to **hibernation**. We have discussed this in many of the *Love of*

Nature books, including those addressing bears and hummingbirds. ***Most animals do not truly hibernate.*** Some go into torpor. Their metabolism and life support slow down, but not to the degree to which an animal goes into true hibernation.

Woodchucks do experience real hibernation. **True hibernation** is a state of minimal activity and metabolic reduction. Hibernation always involves a severe drop in an animal's metabolism to critically low levels. They do not awaken during this state. We find it is a seasonal *heterothermy* characterized by low body temperature, slow breathing and heart rate, and low metabolic rate. It most commonly occurs during the winter months. The North American animals that genuinely hibernate include the ground

squirrel, bats, and woodchucks.[26]

Groundhogs do not eat during hibernation. They use fat reserves built up from overeating during the late summer and early winter months. Before hibernating, groundhogs seal the entrances to their burrow with dirt, maintaining the temperature at a balmy 50°F+ degrees. They curl up into a ball in their leaf-lined hibernation chamber, and their body begins to shut down. They may revise at sporadic and infrequent times, but how long and how often is not fully understood. It is believed that rare awakened activity probably prevents damage to the brain, organs, muscles, and bones from such low blood, oxygen, and nutrition levels. Some have described these rare active awakened

---

[26] See Love of Nature, #7, *Squirrels: Bushy-tailed Scampers* (2020) and #29, *Bats: Most Unique Mammals!* (2022).

moments as a reset button to prevent tissue damage or death.

Miscellaneous

Woodchucks are significant contributors to the ecosystems in which they live. They are considered **keystone species** because more than 100 other species rely on them for their food or shelter needs. They are important prey for the food chain. Keystone species are animals on which other species in an ecosystem largely depend, such that if they were removed, the ecosystem would change drastically.

A Wisconsin study determined that groundhog burrows provide shelter for 20 different species. These included amphibians, reptiles, mice, rats, rabbits, opossums,

Yellow-bellied-Marmot

raccoons, skunks, etc. Some of these animals were often present even while the woodchuck is hibernating. Abandoned dens have become home to otters, chipmunks, voles, shrews, weasels, and snakes. Unused burrows are also enlarged and modified by coyotes and foxes. However, foxes have also been found to cohabitate with woodchucks, sharing the same tunnel system!).[27]

The digging of burrows moves a great deal of subsoil. The process is time-consuming and requires cutting through roots and removing loose rocks and stones as they dig. Besides providing shelters for various animals, woodchucks contribute to the ecosystem by way of **soil aeration**. The multiple benefits of soil aeration are many, including the

---

[27] This is a sensitive relationship as hungry foxes have also been known to sit in wait outside of woodchuck dens awaking their exit.

following:

- Improved air exchange between the soil and the atmosphere
- Enhanced soil water uptake
- Improved fertilizer uptake and use
- Reduced water runoff and puddling
- Stronger turfgrass roots.
- Reduced soil compaction
- Enhanced heat and drought stress tolerance
- Improved resiliency and cushioning.
- Enhanced thatch breakdown[28]

Woodchucks can climb trees. They are quite good at it. This characteristic should not surprise us since they are members of the squirrel family. They will seek tasty leaves and be constantly aware of their surroundings, utilizing

---

[28] See https://www.ryanturf.com/ryan-why-aerate/

trees as a lookout. They are also skillful swimmers.

These shy but slow, stout rodents have many predators. Not only by other animals, but they are hunted for sport in some western states, such as California.[29] Without their keen awareness of their environment and easy access to their dens, they are reasonably easy prey. In the north, badgers hunt woodchucks. Also, do coyotes, bobcats, mink, weasels, and bears. Pups and smaller woodchucks are susceptible to hawks or eagles swooping in from the air.

For this reason, they are seldom seen and prefer to spend time underground and out of sight.

A marmot's average lifespan is 13-15 years, whereas its

---

[29] Some cultures eat marmots believing their fat (also known as *mankei* fat) is a cure for arthritis.

eastern cousin seems to be much less at five to six years. These animals are vulnerable to a variety of intestinal parasites and can carry rabies. But groundhogs, unlike prairie dogs, seem not to experience devastating plagues. However, they are not always welcomed guests by some humans, so they are sometimes hunted or exterminated.

Woodchucks can be considered as pests or vermin when they cause problems or destruction. For example, the woodchuck's burrow systems are regarded as agricultural land problems because farm machines can be damaged when they run over a mound. Ranchers fear their cattle or horses will trip and fall over woodchuck burrows in pastures, injuring themselves.

The yellow-bellied marmot's conservation status and most others are **Least Concern** (on the Internal Union for Conservation of Nature [IUCN]) having a stable population.

Woodchucks might not chuck wood, and groundhogs might not be able to forecast the weather. Still, they are fascinating and essential animals that help make a diverse and healthy ecosystem between ecotones.

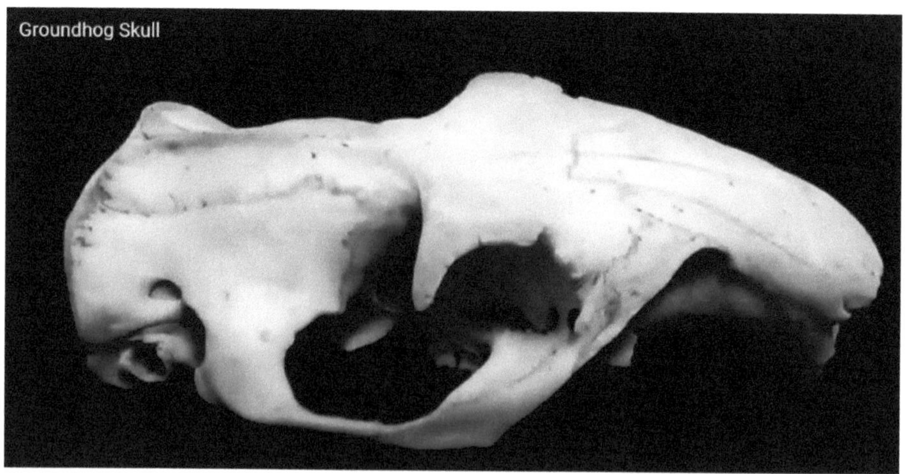

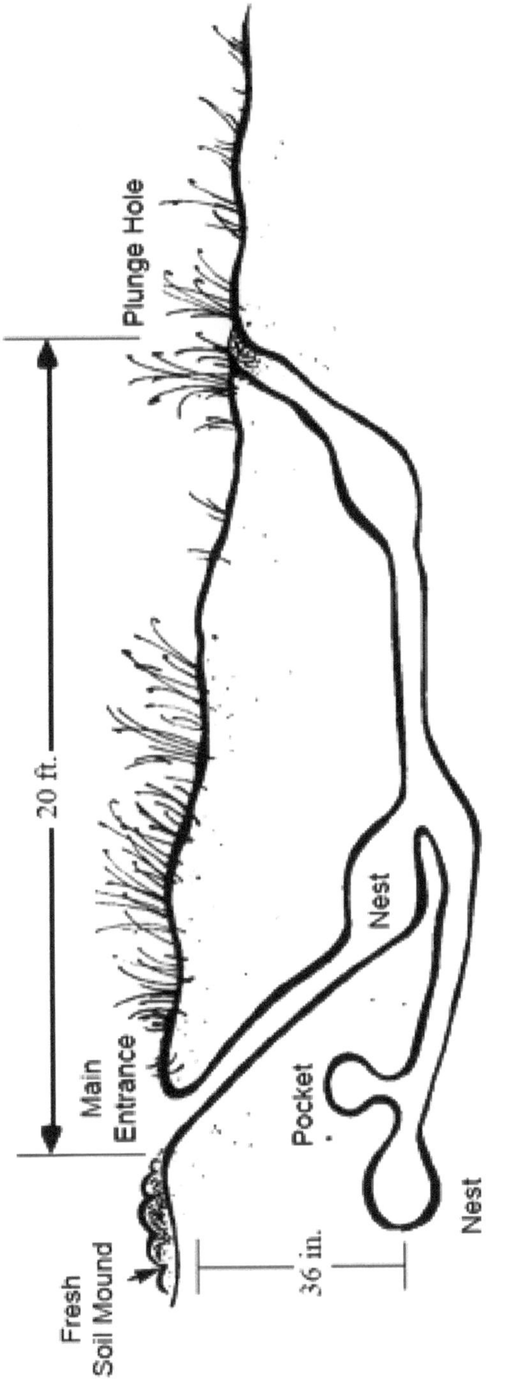

A simplified sketch illustration a woodchuck's den.

REVIEW

1. What are four common names for groundhogs?

2. Woodchucks are mammals. Name four characteristics of mammals.?

3. What cause woodchuck to leave their winter den before spring has arrived?

4. What is *true* hibernation?

5. How does a woodchuck prepare for hibernation?

6. Describe how a she-chuck mother cares for her young.

7. Why would a woodchuck have two dens?

8. What advantages are there to spending most of one's life underground?

9. Why are woodchucks considered *keystone species*?

10. What do you think is a possible explanation of why the western yellow-belly marmot lives longer than the eastern groundhog?

WOODCHUCK

COLORING PAGE

http://www.supercoloring.com/pages/cute-groundhog

Name:_________________

Groundhogs, Woodchucks, and other Marmots

Carefully read each statement or clue. Fill in the correct letters for each box. Use the word bank if necessary.

Created using the Crossword Maker on TheTeachersCorner.net

digging   keystone   cette   solitary   flora   climb   marmots   prognosticator   Marmota

retreat   rodents   weather   Fauna   aeration

Across

1. Woodchucks and groundhogs are ________?
4. Word means 'mountain mouse.'
7. Animal, who's existence enhances the lives of other animals is considered a ________ species.
8. person who foretells a future event.
11. Another name for a burrow or den?
12. Type of animal all marmots are known to be?
13. Another word for plant life?

Down

2. Doing this causes soil to be more absorbent to water and oxygen.
3. 35-40% accurate _________ prediction rates for Punxsutawney Phil?
5. Except for mating season, eastern groundhogs live ______ lives.
6. To 'chuck wood' is actually referring to the woodchuck ______.
9. A groundhogs greatest defense against predators is a fast ______.
10. Like squirrels, groundhogs can also do this?
13. Another word for animal life?

INTERESTING SOURCES TO CONSIDER

Controlling Woodchucks/Groundhogs. Available at: https://youtu.be/7MT31WhXeZQ

Creature Feature: Groundhog. Cleveland Museum of Natural History. Available at: https://youtu.be/UK3pcIIsmfo

Daily Routine of a Cute Woodchuck. Available at: https://youtu.be/f9mejoW0Um0

First Attempt Exploring A Woodchuck Burrow. Available at: https://youtu.be/zuX251iG4lA

Marmot - Groundhog - Woodchuck Call. Available at: https://youtu.be/myXnYqoJ5ag

Marmot Prepares For Hibernation: Winter Wonderland. National Geographic Wild UK. Available at: https://youtu.be/eSTahhfyK8s

Marmots of Olympic National Park. America's National Parks. Available at: https://youtu.be/lJMZV7rYIGY

Priscilla the Baby Groundhog. Sam's Zookeeper Challenge. Available at: https://youtu.be/UYWbqeam8Vw

True Facts about the Groundhog. Available at: https://youtu.be/IANJ9mG8oT8

Why Groundhogs are So Hard to Get Rid of. Available at: https://youtu.be/v0oEzP6kZwU

Wild Groundhog Won't Let Woman Go Home Without Her. The Dodo Wild Hearts. Available at: https://youtu.be/lTafPMOHc7U

Wild Horses Of Payne's Prairie, Fl. Five years of hikes. Available at: https://youtu.be/tgduOSIyTXE

Wild Moments: How Do Woodchuck's Hibernate? Available at: https://youtu.be/vKUtZchAQGQ

Woodchucks: Learn more about these wild neighbors. Available at: https://youtu.be/H44ZkD5rEHk

ABOUT THE AUTHOR

Richard NeSmith is a native of Florida, USA. He grew up wading through the swamps of central Florida with his two younger brothers during the pre-Disney era and unknowingly falling in love with

biology, wildlife, and nature. He has lived in seven American states, twice in Australia and once in Mexico City. He holds eight university degrees and has taught for 14 years in secondary schools, here and abroad, and another 13 years as a professor of science in several American universities, twice University Dean, and online Instructor. He currently heads up a professional development organization helping teachers become more effective. His passion for learning (and *how we learn*) did not develop until *after* graduating from high school. His only explanation for this is that *having a goal made all the difference in the world.* He enjoys reading, hiking, nature photography, golf, tennis, and RV camping.

http://richardnesmith.obior.cc

Applied **P**rinciples of **E**ducation & Learning *presents*

***APE*-Learning**

AMAZON AUTHOR's PAGE:

https://www.amazon.com/author/richardnesmith

Educational, wildlife, and naturalist books
Dr. Richard NeSmith

Paperbacks: http://amazon.com/author/richardnesmith

Issue 1
Raccoons:
Friendly Bandits
Dr. Richard NeSmith

Issue 2
Sandhill Cranes
&
Pileated Woodpeckers
Flaming Redheads
Dr. Richard NeSmith

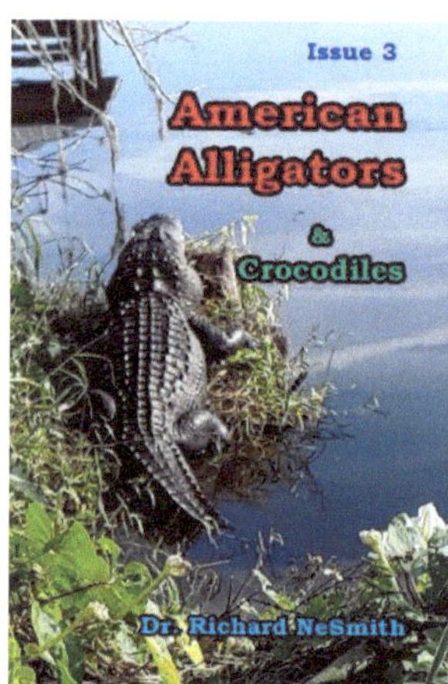
Issue 3
American
Alligators
&
Crocodiles
Dr. Richard NeSmith

Issue 4
Bobcats:
Ghostly Elusive
Dr. Richard NeSmith

Issue 5
Foxes:
Sneaky Rascals
Dr. Richard NeSmith

Issue 6
Armadillo:
Little Armored One
Dr. Richard NeSmith

e-books: https://bit.ly/3iuCgB3

---

[i] Special thanks to the following who kindly provided permission to use their photographs.

From Unsplash: abdullah-ali-aox, Ralph Katieb, Abigail-Lynn S., and Danny Wage.

From Pixabay: RusticPix, pizano13, Avia5, cgordon, Mike Goad, Jason Pinaster, LiveLaughLove, Stefaan Van der Biest, Der Mentor, eliza28diamonds, chrisratzlaff, James LeVos, Amy Moore, Ray Miller, Aline Dassel, Lyn Brattonm, PublicDomainPicture, Mona El Falaky, and Claudio Steward.

From Creative **Commons**: Mousebelt

Finally, *special thanks* to my friend **Stacey Diamond**, for her support and generous sharing of her wonderful nature photographs.

If you enjoyed this book, please go to amazon.com and share a nice review. ☺

Thank you everyone.

Love Learning – Love Nature – Love Life